A Factory Upon Water

Poems 1994 – 2014

Jason Cieradkowski

Paris On The Hudson Publishing

A Factory Upon Water

Poems 1994 – 2014

Copyright © 2015 Jason Cieradkowski.

All rights reserved. No part of this book may be used or reproduced in any manner whatsoever without written permission of the author.

Paris On The Hudson Publishing

First Edition

2015

Cover art by Rosalie Nascimento

ISBN: 978-0-578-15628-6

Then There Is Alone	9
Bluebird Vote	10
Seasoned	11
Two Peppers A Day	12
Kingfisher	13
Spring 67	14
From the Sea	15
1000 Rapiers Found	16
The Surf Speaks winds	17
Reflection of a Birthday	18
Time	19
For The Walk Home	20
Shell	21
A True Passenger	22
All Aboard	23
Going To Bomb The Clinic	24
How You Like Me Now?	25
Midnight On The Farm	26
A New Partner	27
The Obscure Smoke Jockey Clubs	28
What Would You Do?	29
What We Might Do, Say October Second Or Third	30
Will You Be Arriving Soon?	31
Fridays With Pop	32

Written At Public School #6 After An Easter Vacation Spent In Greece   33

Before We Leave The Terminal   34

Picnic Where We Want   35

10:30 Friday Night In a Suburban Neighborhood With Flash Cars In The Driveway   36

To Joy   37

To Be All Farmers Possibly Just In Mall Clothing   38

Three Modes Of Willingness   40

Cottage In Arrifana (for Rosalie)   42

Belfast   43

Bayonne   45

Frigiliana   46

Ogdensburg #82   47

Limerick   48

Waking Up At 3 am.   49

Oslo   50

In 1962 The Tree Was Moved From The Front Yard To The Backyard   51

Jersey City #9   52

3 Stories Upstairs Palisades Avenue   53

The Newspaper Man On Route 9   54

Window 116 Brunswick St.   55

Generality   56

Familiarity   57

The Photographer Was A Painter   58

In The Missoulian Alleyways I Rummaged Through Rummage 59

Lonely In A Western Town 60

Missoula blues #36 61

The If And And Of What 62

Watching The Otter 63

True Beauty 64

A Diversion For The Minute 65

Indecent Love Poem #33 66

A Date 67

Mi Poema Amor 68

Meditation 68

Paradise 68

Reading D.T. Suzuki 69

Shedding 70

Acute Corner Upon Reason 71

Moustacio 72

29 Dead Horses 73

152 Feet Below The Acropolis 74

Black Market Cologne 75

C'est La Vie, Guele De Fuch 76

Charging For Mariscos 77

December Girls, January Love Sexies 79

Dresden 81

El Albayzin 82

Flowers For Catalan 83

For Zofia   84

It Takes Fifteen To Tango In My Book   85

Lips   87

Monkey Lady   88

Morangos Com Acucar   89

Pumpkin as Bait   90

Release The Pulse   91

Danced Like a Demon   92

Sweet Thursday   94

The Essence Of Friendliness To A Polish Girl Written From Spanish Town (Karpinski)   95

The Plastic Bag Is a Savior   97

The Waltz Is Always In Three   98

The World Our Gallery   99

Hi, I'm From A Small Mining Town, Would You Like To Dance?   101

Angels On The Hudson   102

Then There Is Alone

And then there is alone
 like nothing
   in the wind
     and the gusts they start to blow
        right by my love sweet darling

   you can beat your heads into the ground
  maybe make them feel a beat
 something like a rhythm
boom boom
like smoky
  oh so soul deep

     how the hell do you pronounce that?

like church rounds
   walk past lock deep

I lost her at the hip smoke
      when everything was hot and complete.

Bluebird Vote

Bluebird vote
bus in the trucker lane
there is no fear
for we'll pass out all the blame
it will destroy all hope
if that's what you want to hear
bluebird vote
the trucks and the busses are clearing
a path for the people.

Bluebird vote
the pantry is empty now
but have some hope
for we'll cross the border soon
but it will probably be the same
with the luck we've had so far
bluebird vote
please make my decision for me.

Seasoned

Sand evening
and luck struck
nothing down

winter spring
from the fall
summer's pain

lock of eyes
cast in love
no surprise

with evening's glove
mornings night
will be soon June.

Two Peppers A Day

Two peppers a day
and if from the garden
licked meadow down
dew tomorrow's spring

and as if to settle glory
two peppers a day
on earth that is not found
most simplest, thus can be

trodden belly full
thy sights a sullen tree
two peppers a day
warmer days we sing

soon hope a sapling grow
where once a pasture sprang
folly fallowed unfurled
two peppers a day.

Kingfisher

And perhaps it was the covering of the face
yet one cannot deny the simplest of words
of personality
    the somber sea
     our pasts
       candles in the sky
        the excitement of a bird
        the cold unforgiving sea
   binding onto uncommon poles
  it took the dune fence and all
to wrap a wind around our fists
    to no avail, no control.

Spring 67

In the bell tower
from up the spiral
I pulled the rope
the town skipped

opened up ledgers
climbed half up ladder
to signify Sunday
say Thursday perhaps

calloused of course
rouse the rest as they
slumber lay we close
curtain bells we hear.

From The Sea

To bite your neck and taste the races of mankind
upon my tongue my lips moistened now
I forgot who I am in the confines of my shameless self
who covets away the minutes and seconds of the day.

To see the leg of middle age up above each thought
never written to see the preview before it's filmed
before it's stretched out like fish on a string drying
in the sun with the help of salt from the sea.

1000 Rapiers Found

1000 rapiers found
in a chest
  thrust upward
      when snow rebounds
      in the image of tarot
      or perhaps fruity
         or to piss on the trinity
         everything
         bottom of the bowl
         wooden without shine

The Surf Speaks Winds

The surf speaks winds
winds of indiscretion
and they are the winds

They are the winds
of indiscretion
of ovulation

And then
the heart rotates again
and the surf laps

Unto another
the muskrat dies
and goes to sleep

Upon the beach
dead, drop bodied
furry tail, yellowed teeth

Reflection of a Birthday

    The can wasn't there
        nor was the narwhal picture
            June 1955 someone's parents

    the Tlingit chapter book
        was opened to the pinnacle
            therefore upon reading

1976 the meadows of skyland
      (forgot but wanted)
          to carve the names in the wood

The can was half empty the hand
      held on to (the grasp) clenched
          in more words than one

in more fields of folly heather plenty
      purple, your parent's songs
          forever vesting while in womb

Time

Under the m and e of time

It might be hard to find

The combination of one

And the solution for some

Under the m and e of time

There is no time for t

Don't worry for the i

There are new days for some

Under the m and e of time

For The Walk Home

The harvest moon
over king's purple
field's threshing
reaping under the
wind bent birch

A plover call? A
black bird perhaps
in distance a tractor
shuffling of the dead
branches like bees

pain de campagne
a little sweat from
brow earth in mouth
from hand to face
bitterness of a gnat

fire in the distance
freshly chopped wood
diesel from trucking
the wheat and grape
smoke caps the night

the bark of the birch
sun caked forehead
plucking a plume of
bulgur wheat to stick
between my teeth

Shell

Propane tank on the deck
tossing it over onto the rocks
by the little creek
in the backyard

Explosion! What did you expect
it to do?
Roll down the hill
lodge itself along the bank?

Among the plastic plant pots
cold November turtles.

A True Passenger

My brother rides a motorbike
through the city of Cincinnati.
A book about world war two
propaganda posters
like the "We can do it!" ones
which hung in all the factories
showing the woman
flexing her biceps
silently rests
in the side car.

All Aboard

Sometimes I like to paint
people on cardboard
gathered from the alleyway.
I take anything that's not strapped
down. We pardon ourselves from this
kind of thievery. If you don't like
it, then you're not one of us.
Dancing around the room I look
at them and laugh. I pretend I'm
you, I pretend I'm me, my peoples,
my faces, keeps me company at night.
In the apartment the lights are on
and the curtains are closed. A voice
inside, whispering. I listen, I can
talk to them if I want. Sometimes I
touch them and move them around,
and ask them:

Will this train take me anywhere?

Going To Bomb the Clinic

Waiting for the payment,
the keys, the airport
locker number, # 89
Newark international, it
was an easy job, nobody
expected it to blow up
too soon.

The car was flame
by exit 12 on the
Turnpike, the body
a carbon burnt black
with teeth grinning
still in perfect form.

The Christians down
south said it was a
bible like catastrophe.
Us northerners figured
it was god's best choice.

How You Like Me Now?

Sometimes you can't

help but wonder

or wish to be

tied up

restrained

and denied access

then you realize

such things as

the vastness of pleasures

and the deliberate

actions that others

pursue

not to mention

the things that

ones don't know

such as:

would I look good in leather slacks?

Midnight On The Farm

In the farm house lies

chickens

cocks

and hay

horses outside

to eat it

and

daughter in the loft

with lover

and whiskey

sowing.

A New Partner

Somewhere
     my wife friend
and   companion
    rest
drinking beer in her
       back   yard
azaleas and rhododendrons
blooming
you're sunning in the
after
noon
you're baking
      back is red turn
over
upward   not a cloud
in the sky
a six foot brown
wooden   fence
encloses you
from the eyes
                    outside.

The Obscure Smoke Jockey Clubs

And when I escape from everyone
I go home
and dance
to Turkish belly dancing music,
the neighbors don't seem to mind
so I usually don't stop until sun
rise, oh
if I were only spotted
maybe I could achieve recognition
for such a pure form
of foolishness.

What Would You Do?

At a Georgetown cafe
I eat Greek pastries
at a sidewalk table
admiring the floral arrangement
in front of me.
At half wilt it bellows
"kiss me!"
so I kiss the middle
and gather a scent.
Then it says,
"Rip my petals off!"
so I tear and remove them
dropping half on the table
and half on the floor.
As I sit holding the stem
petal-less bloom it says;
"Eat me!" so I eat the whole flower
and how good it tasted.

What We Might Do, Say October Second Or Third

Could you come into my garden and
ferment,
   could you come
   into my garden

     there is lighter fuel
and rakes in the garage
(You want gloves?)
                      OK

looking in the boxes
looking on the shelves
       matches next to the can
       third shelf.

And to see you
   dousing the forget-me-nots
and asters,
        mud on your face

blowing a kiss my way
  after I throw the match
      setting a flame
      all that was spring.

Will You Be Arriving Soon?

Drinking orange pekoe tea and
eating lemon poppy muffins
on a wintry Sunday afternoon
with you
is not truthful.
Instead
in my cup
is Earl Grey tea
the muffin I bought was dry
it crumbled when I took a bite
and I'm reading
John Donne.

Fridays with Pop

On Fridays I still wait for my father to call
but he's dead and he will never call on Fridays again.

I wait, humoring myself with cold beer
recalling all things I would have told him about my day

a little laughing, engaging complaining
cursing never planning more daydreaming toward death

my brother talked baseball but I talked about
leaving the damn country hell I would've moved with him to

Guatemala, Santo Domingo, Hong freaking Kong
I could have been born in Barbados god dammit how I wish!

but never a chance taken never seized a reverse
carpe diem perhaps fuck the day and screw it up as best you can

wake up go to factory stay in factory eat breakfast
lunch and never leave the factory till last worker leaves but you

never left did you dad? You died on the cutting
room table like a pattern destined for Chinatown on a box truck

graffiti says born and died in Passaic, glue factory
90 Dayton Ave all things stubborn and sticky, Boxer's cement.

Written At Public School #6 After An Easter Vacation Spent In Greece

My calloused hands (though not calloused now)
    anymore, from fifteen years onward sweeping garment floors
        tying bundles of dresses and blouses
            are lost as I look now
smoothing out the years
    I wish for these hands back when I see
retired Greek sailors building walls
        and the ones still bringing in the catch
the cats coming down hills into the harbor
    like clockwork
            their fur soft against their hands
                the difference in texture
                      lifestyle
my calloused hands are calloused no more yet in mind still
    tough enough to pull on rough twine
        and as to not rip the skin in one last tug
I use them to wave a gesture toward someone potential who might
    be interested in such a history of hands
    work years displayed
        they are shown
            extended when language interrupts and
                      disallows

        extended as if
                      to say:

        Take them!
    I can trace them on paper and send them to you through
    the mail
                    after we
                    part.

Before We Leave The Terminal

"It's like hanging outside a foreign airplane terminal, they first lay eyes on you, then you can make a move."

"You can go out for a drink.

or better yet, room and board them."

"But of course.

The nearest international airport is over 3 hours away

vapor trails trick magic

the crowd is astonished with amazement

somehow gasped?"

Picnic Where We Want

And in that soft forgiving voice
    even with nothing for which to forgive
    and the Manhattan hair-cut
    by which you now carry

    visions of the south of france
    train stations and cafes laughing
    in the boulangeries every morning
    except the nights when we leave a note

on le poste box:
> *deux chocalatains*
> *deux croisants avec beurre*
> *une bauguette campaigne*
> *Merci, Anaisse*
> *Les Americains*

and the rooster crowing as we hear
the car pull up and everything under
tires then tea from a bowl-shaped cup
an embrace with pastry in our mouths
envisioning a map the realization
we are here and the others
back home in new jersey among
sweltering heat and american curse words
summer thunderstorms and small portions
of foul-tasting food

      we can pick our own fruits on walks
    and picnic where we want

10:30 Friday Night In a Suburban Neighborhood With Flash Cars In The Driveway

The sluts are in the belfry and the cops are outside shaking up the neighborhood with nightsticks and flashlights.

Anticipating the knock of the hand on the pantry door, the promiscuous huddle together like young eye-less bunnies.

To Joy

To joy he climbed the ledge
topping what he'd done before
(they'd done before)

stretch it out on the water's quay
for there will be no spilling

for are they behind, "Are they
behind?" waved on to joy

with the thumb and index finger
fixed the sway of your torso

Oh Christ ye climb for olives
ya climb with the people behind

you's are all one like olive
meat, pit and rind.

To Be All Farmers Possibly Just In Mall Clothing

In the hobby shop he flew planes of wood burlesque beyond
trapeze hooligans with cap guns mimicking movie row.
Georgetown hipster or panic
licking four dollar lips with a gash in your leg
talking to drunk wives wearing zirconium and gold,
peeing outside the Hirshorn
getting your picture taken by four students from Korea
shaking their hands and moving along.
To build a triangle to the sky
     to build a shape for you and never wash thee hands

     from tilling.

Light shine boys shuffling sugar tricks every three corners or so
"and that guy right there, that's Moses, but don't call him that."
I'd say twenty and over - no caps unless one is painting or coating
or shaping or chipping or painting, then a cap would be fine,
say not to get paint in your hair, or wood chips or something.
The cot empty and creaking folded up in the linen closet contains
no linens at all hosting the shepherd's' heroes and woes, cuddling
in the sleeping bag - son of a bitch bastards.
Ramming the iron gates with the car to get out of the Massachusetts cemetery
     December thirties

    with this; to till from.

Even a workhorse paradox, or say surrounded in canvas
so as not to see, will hinder a lunch-in, sit down rest in the bushes
along side a tree - maybe birch - maybe pine - nonetheless bark
lining the corridors, lining the ways - lining - "line em up!" - lining.
Girlfriends getting pierced in South Dakota, boyfriends dancing
drunk with women from Oregon spilling sounds of lust - leather
short cuts, in the park on the see-saw, outside of the porno shop
seeking blondes named Mary and deciding whether or not to put oneself
in dangerous situations, running with the rebels in America central
    drinking the rivers dry

    clearing to till.

Three Modes Of Willingness

I. Jersey City New Jersey USA

Singing rocknroll songs
out the window

as if within a turret
you can say

you are anywhere
but you're still going to be

where you are it's
someone's birthday

II. St. Salvey Lisle Sur Tarn France

Riding the bicycle
alone along

fields of sunflower
km's of vineyard

the arcade and
wash pool

with North Africans
sitting down to picnic

III. Hydra Greece

The Albanian children
walking up

hundreds of stairs
from school

near port on the walk
a volleyball

bounces over the fence
into my hands

Cottage In Arrifana
(for Rosalie)

Through the kitchen window
in Arrifana just left of the
shower you sautéed garlic
and peppers your face in the

window Atlántico straight
view outside the grill fired
chorizo from Aljezur and
dorado fresh from backyard

wood burned all night waves
crashed and grew while moon
rose upon Iberian cliff soon to
be in the sea as the day grew

Belfast

(1)

Not in a black
taxi watching
at red light

against brick
wall man beating
shit out another

light green we
drove off speech
less to Irish Sea

(2)

Walking out in
evening the pub
east toward lit

windows turning
left to the revolving
barrel British tank

stopped dead rotation
continuing back track
wooden swing doors

(3)

inside an Italian man
with bulbous tipped
fingers held them up

talking about picking
apples all day for a
meager sum of pounds

after midnight a bum
waited outside a pizza
shop waiting to pounce

Bayonne

a blue and yellow stairwell
leading to a flat double the size
of a wash room

dancing in the square
ETA bar playing reggae
thinking I'm French I wait

waiter bop pops the cork
tossed in the alley with the others
I wanted to kiss a stranger on the bridge

I crossed it alone, the Nive?
I saw us sitting at this quaint café
where the lights chatted conversations

across the river, we were never there
up from the tides this city floating
on water.

Frigiliana

the wooden table drums
refracted down the valley
so much more car off cliff

dog chase actually tackle
not us after slurp under door
open window new cats clothes

on rooftop to luna up the street
beso me mucho the entire town
now awake because of us

Ogdensburg #82

The house was held together
with string and wishful thinking
allusions to other's lives
illusions, delusions, fiction

trees that hid the shame are
gone now replaced by unkempt
rhododendrons and azaleas
no place left to run away

the mailbox has no number
the postman knows, holidays
come and go celebrated never
near, an empty box of wine

scented candles masking shame
doors never opened windows
same grass will always grow
weeping willows fall new place

to hide near exposed rock
an old rusty mailbox, badminton
net from the 80's and a cement base
from a Jonny Bench batter up game.

Limerick

My legs dangled from the bar
in stab city watching a table
of hairdressers light wood top

the pedestrian center cold
metal night fall fast blinked
shoppers strolling home

flight attendants putting
the Smiths on the jukebox
It's suddenly 1987 and I smile

Waking Up At Three am.

Pedro shouted that their cocks had lost,

back alleys of paradise,

blood and beaks

all seven of them,

southern Tijuana

Feb.

1966.

Oslo

the Scandinavian one was petrifying
the house was too

I made the sign of the cross
about 8 times today

eating lamb's eyeballs
with 4 fingers

In 1962 The Tree Was Moved From The Front Yard To The Backyard

The lone pear, 25 feet up or so
                         suspended in
      Hudson county sky
            small and young

light green   un-nibbled
               for the nibbler has yet come.
Who's in the shadows behind the garage?
                who's squawking like sickened sparrows?

When the blue is up in Jersey city
     we can assume the Mexican is selling flowers
   the harbor a sailing mess
                 Miss liberty is scared!

One pear on one tree
              one damn pear
as small as a buffalo's earlobe
                one pear green.

The sunflowers across the street have taken all the rays
      droughting the pear
                skinning the nibbler
recuperating in the old garage with the rusted rakes and Chevy.

Jersey City #9

Stacking rocks
      in the backyard where I once
            fell in love
 with a lady
      a fair   circus lessons (not
            given here)
there the angels ride motorcycles in moving
  cylinders
            some people learn things
  like that
    (other things too)

3 Stories Upstairs Palisades Avenue

3 stories upstairs I used to wonder
why each light was on

maids? late nights? negligence?
burglars? white collar crooks?

I always settled on infidelity as
it helped me sleep

moreover someone else's pleasure
was better than my solitude

you'd come and go as lights would
turn on and off in my bed

through window your fictions
tricked and sought me

to the next day each told
filament a soul gutter wash

The Newspaper Man On Route 9

I gave him fifty cents for the journal
he said, "Thank you," and took the
25 cent pieces into his gloved hand
before turning back at me to ask:
"Am I bleeding?"

Window 116 Brunswick St.

The way the light kisses the coast goodbye
yellow off metal with orange from Newark

From the third floor, chimneys stop cars
and internationals arrive on the fly

A bamboo grows in Jersey City on a
window sill, still warm October, tracing

the outline of building tops, almost pinkish
hue, seeking employment in the early stars.

Generality

Oh Pulaski skyway, are you
my way home?

I could see all faults falling
seek failure to fly Pulaski

listen on the city's esophagus
alongside bleeding rivers

alongside rust belt ruin east
coast righteousness a flip

movie look left right either
way no chance down

no way to right wrongs
to eat iron without reason

Familiarity

And I opened the trunk
and found nothing but
a jack,
some oily rags
and a pair of soiled panties.

So much for the picnic.
Besides I heard it was
going to rain
anyways.

If The Photographer Was A Painter

High shorts anywhere
    constitute 3 glances to the wind
    and calculated arrangements
    (cuddle entangles, thrusts)
    non-existing and secured safely
    in files.

In kansas, california, montana
    rest stops before thunderstorms
    headed eastward, rest stop looks
    (common place anywhere) stretching
    on a hot hood sipping warm
    water.

The person looked like feldspar
    up above the gully, by union square,
    dakota, carolina, canyon de chelly
    backdrops for a mere remembering
    medium for a fact enacted for just
    display.

In The Missoulian Alleyways I Rummaged Through Rummage

dead rose gardens and tin cans filled with lilac leaves

floating among

the water rim

a dog behind the old motor-bike, blue, rusty

with taped up seat

silver

weeds and wildflower growing through the spokes

a blonde reading a book

soups on

the smell poking out

the door wide open

a whistle for tea, a two to be sought.

Lonely In A Western Town

Passing out
next to a college art magazine

from Wyoming

folded out open
to a nude cowgirl.

Missoula Blues #36

Eating ice
cream   waffle
sandwiches   midnight
Saturday.

The moon is a crescent
          missoula in
february it was sunny today
cloudy tomorrow.

I love the way   you
always say   thank you
in Poland   we say '
dzien   ku   je.

We sit
and rest   as the clocks
run
     away.

The If And "And" Of What

Of willow   made of
    soft shell bark
                  sienna
among tannery
              you
always
    in season
  picking
           butter cups
along rivers
        fields of
            canvas.

Watching The Otter

Glistening of the water's crest
upstream past ponderosa
                     the bend
wind carries lodgepole breath
      from atop   a lone

iced over leaf

            another

                    thawed and

passing by.

True Beauty

now that is true beauty
bugged out
like the hair
left
after.

does anybody love her?

you sit there
holding her hair

asking
again

and

again.

A Diversion For The Minute

The curiosity of touch
    or perhaps taste
    the supple suck of a drink together at a dimly lit bar
        years go by and the brushing of conversation persists
        infrequently
        to portray this

        an unwanted wait
        eating croissants with you in the morning
        and the smell of you on my moustache
as I swallow bread.

Indecent Love Poem #33

i love you
why
because i can't

i wondered
always what if
i wrote i love you

in a poem i actually
wrote about someone

i truly loved.

A Date

Empty wine glasses
panties

and

used records
it's over.

Méditation

Je pense a toi
aujourd-hui
je ne sais pas
pourquoi.

Mi Poema Amor

Ella duerme
a alguna parte
        nunca.

Paradise

I am underneath
a pile of books
while you
are calling
my name.

Reading D.T. Suzuki

Green leafed
wintry tree
obstructing view
of
rapid
river.

Shedding

Coming home
with an unraveled
used condom
in his pocket
he discards of it
in the woods
one half mile
from the house
by an old
wooden fence.

Acute Corner Upon Reason

tonight is like cutting sweethearts
like splitting seconds with minutes
like seeking seed in the sky
you try to record life
but fail to see a corner of reason

Moustacio

With the chimney abandoned it leads to nothing at all and to cook with the flame she says "It's 1938, where have you been?"

With the guns and the drugs the pose is now struck, snapshot, smile, and smirk, the flowers are woven, with pulleys to jerk.

Where have you been?

Throwing knives at viente tres.

Hola! Mira! Mira! Es Classico Domingo! Es Classico Domingo! Mira! Mira! Hola! Mira! Buena! Es Classico Domingo!

The furniture's on the rooftops, you throw knives at viente tres, the canaries are in the cage as we kiss the pastries away. And you're wrapped up in your shawl, and oh Moustacio, won't you have one last drink with me? As if you laugh it off with the chimney abandoned it leads to nothing at all and you cook with the flame "It's 1938" she says, "Where have you been?"

29 Dead Horses

Five years of work and I'm still not fed
I've got teeth falling at my feet
Send the letters to lost souls
Flip the coins in between your fingers
Take down the institution
Abandon your intuition

Five years of work and I'm still not fed
And I hope you die for the same reasons I die
Because we're bastards
We'll die separately for sure
I hope that's the way
And I won't celebrate a day for you

152 Feet Below The Acropolis

And her essence reminded me of walking down the avenue on market day
where they wrapped everything up with a heart-felt desire
and the peddlers yelled out, and we walked down unknown avenues
past kiosks, abandoned cafes, Greek theater, comedies, original I guess.

152 feet Below The Acropolis that's where we met

And she sat in the corner of the café reading her book softly sipping her little drink
and lightly lifting our heads every twenty five seconds or so our eyes would meet
and then I approached her and I tried every language I thought I had known,
not one of which she knew and she shrugged and looked at me with those refugee eyes, the eyes that I love.

And after unknown gestures were given I gave her a piece of paper on which was written the address of where we could meet the very next day, and that day did come and across the room our eyes would again connect but the crowd was too large to get close again to the those refugee eyes, the look that I love, those refugee eyes.

152 feet Below The Acropolis that's where we met.

Black Market Cologne

Black market cologne

Black market cologne

Black market cologne all the ladies are waiting for you tonight

I'm on my way and she follows

I'm on my way and she follows

I'm on my way out of the place where they sell

Black market cologne

Black market cologne

Black market cologne all the ladies are waiting for you tonight

He says, "Hey you want something special? Do you want what a lady wants tonight?"

I'm on my way and she follows out of the place where they sell.

Things never change, no they never, no they never change

not for five dollars, no, not for five dollars

Black market cologne

Black market cologne

Black market cologne all the ladies are waiting for you tonight

They're on the platform and they're waiting for the train to come.

You're at your house and you're waiting for the ladies to come.

C'est La Vie, Gueule De Fuch

Down the avenue she walked alone
she had no control, she had no control

She got on the boat and she sailed away
away from shore, away from shore

And she waved goodbye from distance on deck
away for sure, away for sure

And with her hands in the air kilometers away
the weeks run long, the weeks run long

Charging For Mariscos

The single lady in the hills
    she is down in the valley
    and I offer her my love
        she has two bottles of
      water for me

and a loaf of bread
  and a smile that I want to
      I want to dance off with
     I want to dance off with you

and as the snow falls
down in sizes
    more grand than usual
    upon this city
       these streets where we
      walked images unseen

discard in this city
walking with new thirst
   every few blocks or so
   passing them by
  regardless of their desire

the bar you walk by always has a

few customers
    and they thrive on lost dreams
under the snow they search
        no gloves
           and their fingers don't tingle
              not now no more!

They glow with their envy
            the others live their lives

        It will take years to scatter
      and bury these new hopes
    they leave patterns in the snow
        waiting for someone to step on
and crush them forever.

December Girls, January Love Sexies

Switched back 22 miles outside of Broadus, Montana
the air cold, the night thin and your legs dangling.
I had heard once that the Black Hills are spooky
I didn't see them so I couldn't tell you if she was right.
It felt good to cross the river, it always does, everyone's waiting
and the pubs are filled with women who I can scream at
I'll sneak in through the back and surprise them all.

There's a sweet little girl I know from Virginia
she comes up to my chest and I could probably throw her around
while she tries to hang on for her own good.
Her hair is straight, dirty blonde and it always smells like fruits.
It might be said that this could be another fruits and love sexy.

At the pub I couldn't help but give those Times Square sex looks
the band was bad, they must've been from the country.
I kept buying you drinks and brushing your leg under the table
you kept smiling and the barmaid looked like one of my friend's sisters
long and slender sleek and fast.
Everyone would like it, I told her that and she asked if it was like a freak show.
I told her "Maybe but let's not jump ahead of things this train ain't rolling yet."
We wasn't even out of the pub yet, "and I haven't even touched my tickets."

Penn Station man says, "Yeah, yeah we'll take it, we'll take it outside. I haven't, I haven't beat someone's ass in a long time!"

My bags aren't heavy and the petty thieves walk by
they look at me I tell them with my face do stay away
ain't getting in my pockets, ain't getting in my pockets.

To the girls more interesting I guess.
The coughing in the bathroom always relates to junk and the man watching you always use the phone is stealing your credit card number I'm sure you can't be happy with this.

It's on my mind all the time
and I saw the rubbing of the legs on the way to the bus terminal
and I guess it just felt good to see someone else getting touched.
Touched. Touched.
Touched. Touched.
Touched. Touched.

Dresden

Walking through Dresden
the Colombian looking for the German
back from Guatemalan holiday hey.

Wine from the Rhine
pilsner from the Czech Republic
walking through Dresden.

Black leather pants on her
brown leather on him
doing laundry in places where

where you don't live
trying to stay clean.
Love is like a map

you don't know where it's at
you can't find yourselves
because you're not with each other.

I went north, west, east, and south.
Walking through Dresden
with a bottle of wine in your hand

wine from the Rhine.
Walking through Dresden
I reach out and take your hand.

El Albayzín

On my moto
3am.
galloping,
gallanting,
wanting to wind up
down
deed in hand
dire howl scowl
of the dog
you just left,
go and leave
your history
behind

and she walked down the stairs past the muscatel jug big and round like for a last supper after the rains when the arroyo became a little mojado it dribbled some of the mountains down into the sea

You are dirty in front of god waiting for rations that never come from all his children.

Where has your history gone?
Stored in caves and faces of drunk kings and queens

Flowers For Catalan

Did you come over the sea?
Did your star burst in conclusion?
Hey, smile, we're dying every day

And you drift into the painting
It's better there you say
Hey, smile, we're dying every day

With your feet up on the bar top - touch the line
With your feet up on the bar top - feel the line
Hey, smile, we're dying every day

Flowers for Catalan

On alternate days, I see but do not hear
I hear but do not see, I see but do not hear
Hey, smile, we're dying every day

Flowers for Catalan

We can dance, we can dance, we can dance the days away

For Zofia

You can water this down
some say water the life
you can talk to them
somewhere in the back
pages of history books
sitting on sills of desolation.
And this city's gone bust
the change has come
this table is still waiting
to be cleaned up
like a petal that you picked
threw to the wind
a laugh from the past
into the present
like a move to the switch
the switch to the find
it will knock that love
right out of you.

It Takes Fifteen To Tango In My Book

Don't blow me away
it takes fifteen to tango in my book
what book do you read anyway?

You can't hold down these truths
better than you can a bottle of wine
You have diamonds for eyes tonight
and you stare at the ground
I can push you up against a wall but what good would that do?

And you shove it away

It takes fifteen to tango in my book
what book do you read anyway?
There were times when
I thought we were both dead
then your hold would awaken me
and you say that the devil's got you by the ropes he's gonna drag you down tonight
drag you down tonight
you swear that the devil's got you by the ropes he's going to drag you down, he's gonna drag you down

And you shove it away

It takes fifteen to tango in my book
what book do you read anyway?
You got diamonds for eyes tonight
and you stare at the ground

And you shove it away

Lips

"I like your lips, I like your hips
but probably not as much
as I like your lips. I like your eyes,
I like the backs of your thighs,
the bottoms of your feet and the wear that they show.
I like your hair, I like your rosy, rosy cheeks,
but probably not as much as I like your
lips."

Monkey Lady

They say she's getting closer, getting closer everyday.

They say she might be found perhaps it's easier this way.

The talent might equal attention perhaps what is said can be done and the patience isn't over and she waits like someone.

She's swaying on the trees from her childhood climbed and conquered.

She comes out of the hills, into the valleys and into the city.

I saw her walking outside the old communist gardens.

I saw her walking down old dictator square past the lovers almost coitus.

They say she's the monkey lady, some say she's coming back, some say she's leaving.

Some say she's not from here, some say she's not from there.

They say she's the monkey lady she's coming everywhere.

Meeting her is like playing fútbol on ice everything just slips away.

Climbed and conquered the hills must be trampled down and then they turn into cities.

They say she's the monkey lady they've seen her in cities and towns.

She travels by train everyday.

She'll dance wild dances for you if you ask her in the right way.

She'll climb all over you and take you to places you've never been.

They say she's the monkey lady that's what they say.

Morangos Com Açúcar

Put your worrying to the side don't cry daddy won't care anyway
go ahead keep humiliating me I'll sit in this chair and not say a thing
I don't mind with no belly full I'll put my head down until it's time to go
ignoring your manly smirk and remarks I'll just dream myself away in the dark

When you make me cry I want to fly away
don't worry about those eyes
you'll be home for sugar and strawberries

Fuck you and your ice cream too

I just won't eat anything
I just won't say anything (at all)
I just won't love anything
I just won't be anything (at all)

Pumpkin as Bait

And we wait with the pumpkin as bait
for the people who've had enough of talking
tinker tune the hours till tomorrow
I will count them down till I see your face
and we wait eating pumpkin as bait
not the season now
the majority of people in the town
will chase something else
then we'll laugh alone
eating pumpkin as bait

Running through the tracks over tracks
and the trestle it towers Domingo
and the sinker is just a paradise plane away
and the hours are chasing Domingo

get away, get away, get away, get away.

Release the Pulse

The endless empty rooms
the cart with books to the brim
tipped over left to kick
down empty hallways
into new hands
unto others
the carts they wash away
the bricks will tumble down
and in the morning
there is one in your pocket
filled with new masters
the bricks they've tumbled down
that solid hollow sound
and in the morning
filled with new masters
the bricks they've tumbled down
that solid hollow sound

Release the pulse

I thought reflections were free

Dance Like a Demon

She said, "Yes, hello, I'm going to Spain alone."
"Alone?"
She said, "Yes, hello, I'm going off alone."
"Alone?"

And then I envisioned her dancing, like celebrating a goal
in the stadium that was built for her
I had no answer accept for a stare

She said; "Yes, hello, I'm going to Spain alone."
"Alone?"
She said; "Yes, hello, I'm going off alone."
"Alone?"

and I fell back inside her garden
in the skin that I had once known
and she danced just like a demon
and she danced off alone

Somewhere outside the Bernabeu
in the streets of Madrid

She said she's leaving it all behind

She's said she's leaving it for the wolves

and she danced just like a demon

and she danced off alone

Sweet Thursday

Did you get the locket I sent you?   Yes

And the days are falling down like sunsets on a frown

as you cover up your eyes, no water, no tears, no lies, not quite, not yet, not yet not now.

And I sent it in the mail, and the calendar it hangs down, but all I saw was sweet Thursday, and I don't know when that is.

Did you get the locket I sent you?   Yes

The Essence Of Friendliness To A Polish Girl Written From Spanish Town (Karpinski)

What is not true love but drinking and crying?

A look of open hope, your nose against your fabricated wall

yet all so true I know for I am too a builder.

To grab onto one's wrist and squeeze tight to control

another person's flow or a pinched ass not sexual

more like a prick or thorn scratched from running through the woods

catching your breath on an old maple log watching the bugs under the moss

maybe wiping a brow once or twice everyday before you go to bed.

Most of the times non-amused nor laughable anymore, beside the bed;

seven pairs of shoes.

All is golden and everything can yield wheat

like when a certain something stays around

a scent or a piece of paper from someone past. "Esehe or taesehe?"

An old indian asked me after I split a six and told him

about cops and queens and things.

"The sun or the dark sun moon?"

"Could she be both?"

"Hestenov."

"What?"

"The universe."
"Yes, that's right."

A dream where you are wearing an eagle on a t-shirt somewhere in the Appalachians, early spring or summer with the smell of fire in the air grabbing my-hand jumping rocks, "Tasoom."
The indian said, "La alma?"
"The soul?"

Her shoes were covered by flowers.

The Plastic Bag Is a Savior

The plastic bag is a savior
The plastic bag
It crosses through the Kasbah
It crosses through
Looking out over Dar Nour
Looking out over Dar Nour
North African finger hold
North African hold
Fly upon Andalusian wings
Gusts of Sahara origin
Jaunt towards Place du Tabor
Looking for 116 Dar Nour
In and out from under blocks
Medina purchase midnight
Bouncing in bucket seats

Guts of chickens, garbage from bags,
Descendents of the plague?

The Waltz Is Always In Three

The waltz is always in 3
the being not necessary
to divulge to lose
drop the deepness down
drowned out in waltz
which is always in 3
whoops it's you not me
and now it's me and you
but the waltz is always in 3
but why not now
when the wielding will fall
gracefully to the floor
we will waltz no more
for the waltzers waltzed
on out the door.

The World Our Gallery

I'll cover you in paint and call you art
the world can be our gallery for us to be displayed upon
I will come into both of your personalities
taste the inside of your installations

the world our gallery to be displayed upon
I'll cover you and call you art
stretch your canvas as far as it will go
Matka boska trzymaj sie dziewczyno!
tak, cicho!, nie

I've tasted the inside of your installations
where both personalities were waiting
unlocked, displayed, for the world now
I've done what I've done
and now we need to be cleaned

because we are on display
covered and called art
Matka boska trzymaj sie dziewczyno!
tak, cicho!, nie

And you suck it down like it was yesterday
just one more time for old times sake that's what you say

we'll abandon these desires on the city highways
we'll abandon everything in the city alleyways
that's what you'll do we'll abandon everything
tak, cicho!, nie

Hi, I'm From a Small Mining Town, Would You Like To Dance?

Seeing someone everyday
like bats see dark

killing yourself with wonder
through amazement

putting the theory of magnets
to test and living and waiting

creeks occasionally dry up
sometimes precious found

shining like the tip of
a foil

even iron ore after a rain
shows capability

after it's kicked a few times
and the leaves are brushed off.

Angels on the Hudson

Light in the kitchen
shadow behind le musique
an off white wall
      shadow puppets
   angels on the Hudson.

www.ingramcontent.com/pod-product-compliance
Lightning Source LLC
Chambersburg PA
CBHW032058150426
43194CB00006B/567